Happy Birthday,

Love & God Bless You,
Carole ☺

"5-15-13"

THE SECRET TO
Living IS
Giving

MAC ANDERSON

Copyright © Simple Truths 2012

Published by Simple Truths, LLC
1952 McDowell Road, Suite 300
Naperville, Illinois 60563
800-900-3427

Design: Simple Truths Designer: Lynn Harker
Photos: Shutter Stock and ThinkStock

Printed and bound in the United States of America

ISBN 978-1-60810-186-3

01 WOZ 12

TABLE OF CONTENTS

INTRODUCTION

One of my favorite things to do is waking up early on Sunday morning, getting the Sunday paper, making a hot cup of coffee, and kicking back to read about what's going on in the world. It's my quiet time ... my time to reflect and relax.

One Sunday morning about halfway through my little ritual, I spotted a headline that caught my attention, "Graduating Student Credits His 'Angel' " ... and I began to read.

A young man who was graduating from college told the story about how Oral Lee Brown was his "Real Life Angel." In 1987, Brown, a real estate agent in Northern California, saw a young girl in her neighborhood begging for money.

When she went to the school the girl had claimed to attend, Brown couldn't find her, but that day she made a decision that would change the lives of many other children forever. She adopted an entire first-grade class in one of Oakland's lowest performing schools, and she pledged that she personally would pay for anyone who wanted to attend college.

This would be a great story even if Oral Lee was independently wealthy; however, it is a much greater story considering she was a former cotton picker from Mississippi, making $45,000 a year and raising two children of her own.

Brown lived up to her pledge. Since 1987, she's personally saved $10,000 a year while raising donations for her "adopted first-grade kids." And because of her tremendous act of unselfish love, children who could have been "swallowed by the streets" are now graduating from college to pursue their dreams.

We all seek our purpose in life. Most of us wonder how we can make a positive difference during our brief time on this earth. But Oral Lee Brown discovered the simple secret…GIVING. Arthur Ashe said it best,

> *"From what we get, we can make a living.*
> *What we give, however, makes a life."*

That's what this little book is about … how you can find *joy, happiness* and *purpose* in your life by serving others. This reflects the amazing paradox of giving … *you can never help another person without helping yourself.*

It is my hope that these wonderful stories about people, and how they made a difference through giving from their hearts, will inspire you to do the same.

It can change your life … and the lives of others.

All the Best,

Mac Anderson

Joy Boomerangs:
HOW GIVING TOUCHES YOUR HEART

Looking for a guaranteed road to happiness?

It's really quite simple ... give to others. Make a difference in the lives of others and your own heart will be touched in return.

Take the experience of Dr. Howard Kelly in a true story called *Paid in Full*:

One day, a poor boy who was selling goods from door-to-door to pay his way through school, found he had only one thin dime left, and he was hungry. He decided he would ask for a meal at the next house. However, he lost his nerve when a lovely young woman opened the door.

Instead of a meal, he asked for a drink of water. She thought he looked hungry and so she brought him a large glass of milk. He drank it slowly, and then asked, "How much do I owe you?"

"You don't owe me anything," she replied. "Mother has taught us never to accept pay for a kindness." He said, "Then I thank you from my heart." As Howard Kelly left that house, he not only felt stronger physically, but his faith in God and man was strengthened also. He had been ready to give up and quit.

Years later, that young woman became critically ill. The local doctors were baffled. They finally sent her to the big city, where they called in specialists to study her rare disease.

Dr. Howard Kelly was called in for the consultation. When he heard the name of the town she came from, he went down the hall of the hospital to her room. Dressed in his doctor's gown, he went in to see her. He recognized her at once. He went back to the consultation room determined to do his best to save her life. From that day, he gave special attention to the case.

After a long struggle, the battle was won. Dr. Kelly requested the business office to pass the final billing to him for approval. He looked at it, then wrote something on the edge, and the bill was sent to her room. She feared to open it, for she was sure it would take the rest of her life to pay for it all. Finally, she looked, and something caught her attention on the side of the bill. She read these words:

"Paid in full with one glass of milk..."

Signed
Dr. Howard Kelly

(Dr. Howard Kelly was a distinguished physician who, in 1895, founded the Johns Hopkins Division of Gynecologic Oncology at Johns Hopkins University. According to Dr. Kelly's biographer, Audrey Davis, the doctor was on a walking trip through Northern Pennsylvania one spring day when he stopped by a farm house for a drink of water.)

"If you want to lift yourself up,

lift up someone else."

~ *Booker T. Washington*

Connecting
HEART TO HEART

Giving only comes from the heart…when one person takes the time to truly see another's needs and respond. Nurses do this on a daily basis, but RN Hannah Fox captures the reciprocal effects of giving when you are *Connecting Heart to Heart:*

He was a very frail man, small in stature, old in years and very ill, but Mr. P had a significant influence on my career as a Nurse. I met him while I was still in nursing school, working as an extern on a renal and oncology floor.

When I first started, I really wanted to be efficient! I had my checklist of things to get done … blood draws, vitals, baths, and getting people up to walk. Mr. P changed my whole perspective on Nursing CARE. He helped me to see the person inside the body and to truly CARE for my patients.

I met this gentleman when I came into his room one day to help him out of bed and into a chair to sit up for his allotted time. We worked together very slowly, step by step, as I guided him along. When he was finally in the chair, I propped him up with pillows under his arms and legs and made sure the pillows were adjusted just right under his head and behind his back for added support and cushion.

Since I had just finished my first year of nursing school, I had learned all the ways you can position a patient in a bed or chair, especially with the aid of pillows. It was exciting for me to take this "task" of getting Mr. P into a chair as an opportunity to put to use what I had just learned in school.

When we were finished he looked up at me with tears in his eyes, and said, "No one has ever taken the time to get me so comfortable sitting in this chair."

Not knowing how to respond, I said, "Oh, well, I'm just doing my job."

Mr. P replied, "No, you spent the time to get me in the chair, AND get me comfortable, and that means you CARE and you're good at what you do." I leaned over and gave him a hug, because I didn't know what else to say in that moment.

The SECRET TO LIVING IS
GIVING

The next day, I was eager to go visit Mr. P because he had really made an impression on me, and I loved feeling that "bond" between us. When I came in, he gave me a great big smile, and we began the process of getting him up in the chair again. When we were done, he told me a story of a beautiful German girl he met when he was stationed in Germany during WWII. He explained that I reminded him of her and then asked if he could sing me a German love song that he had learned to sing for her.

As he sang, I was deeply moved. I remember thinking, "This is why I want to be a Nurse ... for this feeling of *connecting with a complete stranger*, for the feeling of knowing you gave them a bright spot in their day, even if they are struggling." Another nurse came in to hear the song as well and when we left Mr. P's room she told me that he had been a "grumpy old man" before I came.

I can still remember the day I came in and met his family who were all there to say goodbye. He passed away quietly, and once again, I got him cleaned up and comfortable. It was the first time I had to do post-mortem care, but I was honored to do so. He touched my life and influenced how I practice as a Nurse to this day.

Mr. P taught me that it's NOT just about "getting it done." It's about "*connecting heart to heart*" with my patients ... going the extra mile, making them comfortable even if it takes a little more time, and really CARING for them as individuals.

"For it is in giving that we receive."

~ *St. Francis of Assisi*

LEARNING TO *Give*

Sometimes it's the student who is the teacher. Author Paula J. Fox has been a teacher for 30 years, changing the lives of many of her students. But in her poem, "Lessons from a Little Child," Paula shares what she learned from one student ... about the joy of giving:

Lesson FROM A LITTLE CHILD

By Paula J. Fox

A class of three and four year olds
not yet in kindergarten
but one of them taught me a lesson
that won't soon be forgotten

I was teaching them how to show love to each other
and what it means to be kind
a "hands-on craft" was part of the lesson
to impress it on each little mind

As they wiggled and bounced around in their seats
they weren't listening very well
I wondered if they even heard a word
of what I was trying to tell

For the craft, each child was to make a card
as a gift for someone they love
to surprise them with an act of kindness
in a way they'd never think of

I noticed one child who hurried the task
quickly scribbling to finish his card
he sometimes made such a mess of things
and teaching him could be hard

He knew how to push every boundary
and when things didn't go his way
he'd frequently have a meltdown
and ruin everybody's day

He finished his card before the rest
and shoved it into my hand
I figured he didn't have a clue
what I wanted him to understand

Not feeling very kind-hearted myself
I reminded him ... once more
that giving it to someone he loved would be kind
and that's what it was for

With a twinkle in his eye, he smiled and said,
"I know!... I'm giving it to You!"
It took me a moment to comprehend
then I realized ... that he knew!

He knew exactly what he was doing
he had understood every part
more than just following directions
he was giving me a gift from his heart!

My heart exploded with love for this child
and I felt a wave of shame
he knew more about kindness than I did
I had just been playing the game

It's so easy to judge by the outside behavior
whether rules are followed or broken
but the heart of the child is what matters
feelings and words unspoken

No wonder God loves little children so much
with their hearts so fresh and pure
they can teach us a thing or two about love
they know what it is, for sure!

"Today, see if you can stretch your heart and expand your love so that it touches not only those to whom you can give it easily but also to those who need it so much."

~ *Daphne Rose Kingma*

Volunteer:
LOSE YOURSELF IN THE SERVICE OF OTHERS

Mahatma Gandhi once said, "The best way to find yourself is to lose yourself in the service of others."

When you serve others by volunteering, you often find that you *get* more than you *give*.

Statistics bear this out. In a 2010 *Do Good Live Well* survey of more than 4,500 adults conducted by United Healthcare and Volunteer Match, 68 percent reported that volunteering made them feel physically healthier, while 92 percent agreed that volunteering had enriched their sense of purpose in life.

Volunteering can change both your life…and the lives of those you serve. Author Pamela B. Silberman captures her experience of how a pet rabbit allowed her to "speak" a language of love:

THE SIGN OF THE RABBIT

from *Chicken Soup for the Volunteer's Soul*
By Jack Canfield, Mark Victor Hansen, Arline McGraw Oberst,
John T. Boal and Tom and Laura Lagana

"YOU GIVE BUT LITTLE WHEN YOU GIVE OF YOUR POSSESSIONS. IT IS WHEN YOU GIVE OF YOURSELF THAT YOU TRULY GIVE."

~ *Kahlil Gibran*

Eighty-seven-year-old Lucia had the hands of a twenty-year-old woman. Watching her fingers lightly tickling an imaginary stage in front of her, one could barely resist being drawn into her lyrical movements. Those hands always delivered an insightful message. Deaf since the age of three, Lucia was particularly energetic and adept with sign language, her only form of communication.

I visited Lucia at a local nursing home with my pet dwarf rabbit named Cadberi. Pet therapy was a new concept in nursing homes. But Cadberi was a "ham" and loved his "job."

Cadberi understood visitors and instinctively knew their innermost desire to be needed and

The SECRET TO LIVING IS
GIVING

touched. He inspired even the most confused residents who, during Cadberi's visits, sometimes even spoke or responded lucidly. While he lay in many residents' arms or stretched out on their beds, Cadberi had a special bond with Lucia. She was definitely his favorite.

I did not know how to speak sign language. But after a few days, I realized that even if I didn't know the words, our smiles and laughter communicated volumes. I increasingly became more interested in learning and purchased an American Sign Language dictionary. Goodness knows what Lucia was thinking as I clumsily tried to sign back to her. But her bright-eyed smile and fighting spirit always encouraged me even if she had to guide my hands physically until I got the big "Aha!"

We quickly bonded as student and teacher as well as friends and companions. Our visits became the melding of two worlds far apart in time, yet precious in all the knowledge she was giving me. I wasn't sure who looked forward more to the visits—Cadberi or me. Arriving at the nursing home, he perked his ears up expecting his first "client" meeting. Yet when Lucia rolled around the corner while flashing me the sign for "cute rabbit," Cadberi would begin squirming in my arms, preparing to leap into her lap. She was the only person with whom he'd ride on a wheelchair.

"Cute Rabbit" was the first sign I learned, as it was the most repeated in our conversations. This sign of the rabbit became our hello and good-bye, as time went on, it also became my name.

After three years of continuous visits, Lucia never gave up on me nor I on her. Yet I couldn't help but notice the Alzheimer's disease catching up on her bit-by-bit. It broke my heart to see her struggle and sign back the same questions to me with a deeply bewildered effect. I knew the time was coming when Lucia would no longer be guiding my hands in speech, but I would be holding hers in support.

One day I came to visit and found every nursing home volunteer's worst discovery—a stripped empty bed. Seeing no personal effects, I thought the worst. I felt the tears gathering in my eyes. Minutes felt like hours until a nurse filled me in.

Lucia was still alive but had been transferred to a "step-down" nursing home. This was a smaller center that specialized in caring for the more seriously ill, and it was near her daughter's residence.

Impulsively, I called the center. I was told Lucia was unable to leave her bed and could barely recognize family members. Still, I asked if Cadberi and I could come by for one more visit.

Arriving at the center, I was greeted in the hallway by Lucia's daughter.

"It's not one of her good days," she said. "She won't recognize you and can barely sit up."

"That's okay," I replied. "I just want to give them one more chance to visit."

We walked quietly into Lucia's room. She lay still, sleeping in her bed. She was drawn and pale. Only wearing a hospital gown, she didn't resemble the vibrant woman who taught me so much on survival. Yet Cadberi knew. He knew immediately who she was and began his light kicking, trying to let me know where he wanted to go.

In one quick leap, Cadberi lay comforted by her side. Awakening to find Cadberi's warm brown eyes gazing into her own, she smiled. It was the first smile her daughter had seen all week. Their bond was still there. Then amazingly, Lucia raised her hand and curled her fingers into rabbit ears. She wiggled them in an upward curve... "Rabbit."

"Yes, Lucia," I returned the sign. "Cute Rabbit." Lucia smiled again after signing what would be her final words to me. I continued to hold her hand while petting Cadberi with the other until she fell asleep. Two weeks later, Lucia died.

My bond with Lucia was more than a volunteer experience as we connected much deeper than teacher and student, or volunteer and patient. It was the melding of two souls. We had a language of our own with the sign of the rabbit.

Connections like these are part of the joy of volunteering. Sharing your time allows you to make a difference in the world. And … it can make an impact on those who look to you for guidance.

For example, the Corporation for National and Community Service reports that children who have parents who volunteer are nearly three times more likely to volunteer on a regular basis themselves.

In fact, look what some of the youngest among us have already accomplished:

Melissa Poe, age 9, started Kids for a Clean Environment (kidsface.org) as a way to get young people involved in environmentalism. Twenty years later, it's grown into the world's largest youth environmental organization and has helped plant more than a million trees.

Carolyn Rubenstein, age 14, started Carolyn's Compassionate Children (cccscholarships.com) to connect childhood cancer patients with their healthy peers through a pen pal program. It has since expanded to include a college scholarship program for childhood cancer survivors.

David Levitt, age 12, single-handedly founded a countrywide volunteer network dedicated to collecting and transporting food for the homeless. Today his program has been adopted by 200 schools and together they donate a whopping 234,000 pounds of food to local food banks every two years!

from *How to Be an Everyday Philanthropist* by Nicole Bouchard Boles

So, do yourself, your children, and the world a favor. Choose an organization close to your heart and share your time. You'll be glad that you did.

GIVING AND KINDNESS ARE FIRST COUSINS

Ready to change the world? If you want to become more giving, you don't need more money, you just need more kindness—and an hour a week! Author Dr. Lee Jampolsky shows us the way in an excerpt from his book, *Smile For No Good Reason:*

"I don't have time." This is a common response to why one can't be giving in the community. It's no wonder. In the United States today, people work longer hours and commute longer distances than ever before. Many people still make charitable con-tributions with their money, which is wonderful, but few actively give of their time. Imagine the world if everyone devoted just one hour a week to doing acts of kindness.

There is simple wisdom in the saying, "Practice random acts of kindness and senseless acts of beauty."

"AFTER THE VERB

'TO LOVE' ...

'TO HELP'

IS THE MOST

BEAUTIFUL

VERB IN THE

WORLD."

~ Bertha von Suttner

It doesn't matter where you start extending love. It only matters that you see it as much of a priority as all of your other activities. If you spend some time each week giving unconditionally, you will find all other areas of your life uplifted. When you take the time out of your stressful life to give, your whole life becomes less stressful and more purposeful. You are also likely to find the attitude of unconditional giving spreading over to your other activities, bringing increased peace and calm to your life.

Some people find it helpful to have structure in their giving: volunteering with an organization, school, retirement home, hospital or the like. Other people like the adventure of setting out for an hour each week to find someone to give to: perhaps a neighbor doing yard work, a homeless person on a bench, an abandoned animal. It matters little who the recipient is, it is the act of compassion that will heal your life and contribute to the healing of the world.

I had a friend, Max, who died a few years back—well into his nineties. For over fifty years he walked Carmel Beach every morning, picking up garbage. I think he lived so long and with such joy because of those morning walks of service to nature.

It is easy to become hopeless and overwhelmed by all the problems and atrocities in the world. Train your mind to know that extending love makes a difference. Don't just sit and read the newspaper, wondering what is happening to the world. Make a difference by taking an hour a week to make happy news. At the end of the week, if one life on the planet, or the planet itself, feels a little more cared about because of your decision to take the time to give, you have made an invaluable contribution.

"Acts of love
are what will bring peace to
your life and to the world."

~ Dr. Lee Jampolsky

Giving

Donate:
DO WHAT YOU CAN WITH WHAT YOU HAVE

Even in tough economies, the heart finds a way. It isn't the size of the individual donation that matters. It's the spirit behind it that counts. This story, by Gary Sledge from *Reader's Digest*, shows that anyone can be the spark that lights the spirit of generosity:

SPECIAL DELIVERY

Ten-year-old Riley Christensen and her mother, Lynn, were huddled in front of the family computer, checking out models and prices of bikes. "Let's pick one out for Dad's birthday," Christensen suggested to her daughter.

As Christensen scrolled down the home page of the Bike Rack, a shop in their town of St. Charles, Illinois, a video link for Project Mobility caught her eye. She clicked on it out of curiosity. The clip told how Bike Rack co-owner Hal Honeyman had created an organization to provide specially engineered bicycles to people with disabilities. It showed the happy faces of those who were now riding them—accident victims, injured veterans, and children with disabilities, including Hal's own son, who had been born with cerebral palsy.

"I'm going to buy a bike for one of those kids," Riley told her mother. Two days later, she showed Christensen a letter she had written asking for donations: "I think it's amazing for a guy to make bikes for kids who can't walk," the letter said. "I saw how happy a boy was when he got one ... I'm writing to ask for your help."

Christensen was blown away by her daughter's effort, but doubts quickly emerged. The cost of just one of those special bikes could be as high as $4,000. Riley could never raise the money. Nonetheless, her letter went out to 75 relatives and friends. Within three days, checks and cash began arriving. Then word got around about Riley's campaign, and as Christmas neared, more and more donations rolled in. The teen ultimately raised more than $12,000, enough to pay for seven bikes.

The SECRET TO LIVING IS
GIVING

Last Christmas Eve, Riley pulled on a Santa hat and delivered the bicycles to three of the lucky kids: Ava, a 13-year-old girl with spina bifida; Jenny, a 15-year-old girl with cerebral palsy; and Rose, a 4-year-old girl with a rare genetic disorder. "This is the best Christmas I ever had," said Riley.

She and Ava have since ridden together. "When I ride, I like to go fast, get sweaty, and feel the breeze," Riley says. "So does Ava. She pumps with her arms, not her feet, but she really flies."

Riley is determined to keep her campaign going every holiday season. "I want kids to feel the wind in their faces," she says.

"Real generosity toward the future lies
in giving all to the present."

~ *Albert Camus*

MAKE SOMEONE'S DAY

Opportunities abound every day to give to others. You just need to be ready to act on them ... to make someone's day ... and in doing so, to change someone's life. A story submitted to *Random Acts of Kindness* is one that knocks the concept out of the park.

When I was in college, I worked part-time at a sporting good store. There was a kid who would come by two or three times a week to visit this baseball mitt that he wanted to buy. My manager and I would joke about him not only because he was so dedicated and persistent, but also because he had picked the best and most expensive mitt in the store to obsess over.

This went on for months. The kid would come in, and you could tell he was so relieved that the mitt was still there. He would put it on, pound his fist into the pocket a couple of times, and then very carefully put it back onto the shelf and leave. Finally, one day he came in with a shoebox and a smile about eight miles wide and announced that he wanted to buy the mitt. So the manager brought the mitt over to the cash register while the kid counted out a shoebox worth of nickels, quarters and dimes. His stash came to exactly $19.98. The mitt cost $79.98, not including tax. My manager looked at the price tag, and sure enough the number 7 was a little smudged, enough that a desperately hopeful seven-year-old could imagine it to be a 1. Then he looked at me, smiled, and very carefully recounted. "Yep, exactly $19.98." Wrapping up the mitt, he gave it to the boy.

DO NOT GIVE
SO YOU WILL GET ...

One of the most passionate, giving leaders I know, Dr. Nido Qubein, has a life philosophy about giving that I want to share with you. Dr. Qubein is the author of many best-selling books, one of the most sought after speakers in America, the Chairman of Great Harvest Bread and the President of High Point University in High Point, North Carolina. Here's how he feels about giving:

> *"Always give without remembering, always receive without forgetting."*
>
> ~ William Barclay

Nido said, "I believe in William Barclay's words. That's the way I live my life. I give of my time, of my money, of my energy, of my talent.

"SOME PEOPLE GIVE TIME, SOME MONEY, SOME THEIR SKILLS AND CONNECTIONS, SOME LITERALLY GIVE THEIR LIFE'S BLOOD. BUT EVERYONE HAS SOMETHING TO GIVE."

~ *Barbara Bush*

"In doing so, I've discovered something phenomenal:

The more you give, the more you get ...
so long as you do not give so you will get.

"It's all about giving versus giving back; loving versus loving back. It's unconditional. Those who sow abundantly reap abundantly. This is the way I choose to live my life: I invest one third in earning, one third in learning and one third in serving. Many people looking for meaning in their lives find it by losing themselves in causes greater than they are."

DONATE
WHAT YOU CAN

GIVE 'TIL IT FEELS GOOD

The saying goes, "give until it hurts," but author BJ Gallagher shares a personal experience of how to give until it feels good:

Reverend Ed Bacon of All Saints Episcopal Church in Pasadena, California, stood at his pulpit, resplendent in his flowing white robe and colorful vestments. He's a big man with a booming voice and enough charisma to light up the sanctuary without candles. On this particular Sunday, he was practically glowing with joy—energized by his guest of honor, Archbishop Desmond Tutu, the Nobel Prize-winning peacemaker from South Africa.

"Most people say, 'Give 'til it hurts,'" Reverend Ed announced to the standing-room only congregation. "But I say, 'Give 'til it feels good.'"

"IF YOU HAVE MUCH, GIVE OF YOUR WEALTH; IF YOU HAVE LITTLE, GIVE OF YOUR HEART."

~ *Arab Proverb*

The crowd's laughter and applause thundered their approval. The choir burst into song as ushers made their way down the aisles with collection baskets.

This wasn't just any Sunday—and it wasn't just any collection. Archbishop Tutu had come to All Saints to tell us about the latest developments in his homeland. Apartheid had been abolished and the country was now embarking on the long, slow painful journey of healing. A Truth and Reconciliation Commission (TRC) had been established to facilitate the healing process. It was a court-like body, chaired by Archbishop Tutu, which played a key role in the transition of South Africa to a full and free democracy. Anyone who felt that he or she had been a victim of apartheid's violence could come forward and be heard. Perpetrators of violence could also give testimony and request amnesty and forgiveness.

But, as Reverend Ed pointed out to us that Sunday morning, justice isn't free. It costs money to hold tribunals, to handle the paperwork, to underwrite the process of hearings and all the administrative details. So he asked the congregation to dig deep into our pockets and purses, since he was giving all the donations to Archbishop Tutu to help support the ongoing work of the Truth and Reconciliation Commission.

"I've never done this before," Reverend Ed said, "But I'm going to do it today. I am urging to give what you can, in whatever form you can. If you want to donate your car, we'll take your pink slip. If you want to donate your jewelry, we'll take that. If you want to give cash or a check, or even put your donation on a credit card, fine. We'll take it all. We here in Southern California have a wonderful standard of living—we're rich by any standard. So I'm asking you to give as much as you can to the people of South Africa to support their healing and reconciliation. Most people say, 'Give until it hurts'—but I say, 'Give until it feels good.'"

There wasn't a dry eye in the place. We were so moved by Tutu's sermon, so inspired by his moral authority and loving compassion, that we could do no less than give our all.

D O N A T E
with what you have and feel good

As the collection basket made its way toward me I wondered what to do. My business had been slow, so I had no extra money to give. I needed my car, so I couldn't give that. What can I give? I asked myself. I desperately wanted to support this marvelous process unfolding in South Africa. I wanted to contribute something—no matter how small—to the good people half-way around the world.

The collection basket finally came to me and I looked down into it, still not sure what to do. As my hands cradled the basket of love offerings, I noticed that I was wearing a 14K gold and garnet ring my mother had given me on my 12th birthday. Instantly, I knew what I had to do. I took off the ring, put it in the little white offering envelope, and dropped the envelope into the collection basket. Tears of joy streamed down my face as I passed the basket to the person next to me. I imagined the South Africans melting down my gold ring to help pay for their national healing. I was filled with gratitude and happiness to be a tiny part of something so momentous, so important, so essential to humanity.

As I wiped away my tears and joined the choir in song, I realized that Reverend Ed had been right. I gave ... and it felt good.

"THE ONE-A-DAY VITAMIN FOR THE SOUL IS HELPING ANOTHER PERSON."

~ *Stephen Post, Ph.D.*

THE GIFT OF THE GIVER'S GLOW

Excerpted from The Hidden Gifts of Helping
By Stephen Post, Ph.D.

Stephen Post is professor of preventive medicine and director of the Center for Medical Humanities, Compassionate Care, and Bioethics at Stony Brook University. When he and his family encountered a stressful time after a move across country to take a new job, a happenstance meeting helped him discover the power of "The Giver's Glow."

About five months after our move to Stony Brook, settling in to my new work but still struggling to deal with feelings of displacement and loss, I ran headlong into the holiday season. I missed our friends back in Cleveland, our church, the small traditions we'd established over the years. Although our Christmas mantel was decorated with many cards from friends who I know truly did wish us a happy new year, I found myself feeling a bit quiet when all I wanted was to enjoy the holidays. Then one of those serendipitous moments came along that refocused me toward what I knew to be true: that the hidden gifts of helping would far outlast the other gifts these holidays might bring.

During a December train ride on the Long Island Railroad, traveling back to Stony Brook from a meeting in Manhattan, I fell into conversation with my seatmate, Jack, an amiable man some years older than myself. In the sudden intimacy that can arise between strangers who know they will never meet again, Jack told me that his wife of twenty-years had divorced him and that he had been fired from a job he'd held for thirty years, was newly diagnosed with cancer, and was close to running out of his retirement savings because he'd had to spend the money on day-to-day living. The one thing that was holding him together through all this, he said, was a volunteer job he had serving meals at his church's soup kitchen in Port Jefferson. "It's not just that I can't feel really sorry for myself," he explained. "When I put that food on their plate, and I know they're really hungry —they just can't run to the fridge like I can— I can see that I'm really helping someone. Even if they're too exhausted to acknowledge me or say thanks, that's okay. I don't know," he shrugged. "It just makes me feel like I can keep going another day, and things might start to get better. It's odd, but some days I feel better than I ever have."

"Thank you." I felt as if I had been jolted awake from a deep sleep.

"Sure," he said, clearly confused about what I was thanking him for, and why I was smiling. But I felt as though I'd just been handed my first real gift of the season. This man had far more reason than I had to be suffering the holiday blues, yet by sharing his story he had helped me let go of some of my concerns and remember what I already knew: when all else fails, we can still give to others. And doing so will always be our salvation, our re-connection to the world. This phenomenon of "the giver's glow"— I have learned never to underestimate its power.

You've probably seen people waving brightly colored glow sticks at a night-time event, and you may have had the pleasure of experiencing the magic of snapping the tube and seeing it suddenly light up, creating a soft, colorful glow that lasts for hours and can light up your way on a dark night. The principle is simple: the chemicals in the translucent plastic tube mix to cre-ate the glow—but only when you break the tiny glass capsule inside the tube. The brokenness is part of the process, and just as the broken parts of our lives can allow us to reach out to others and create radiance, lighting the way not only for those we serve but also for ourselves and everyone we meet.

There are always ways to reach out to others, even if money is not abundant. *Experience Life*, the magazine of LifeTime Fitness, published the following "Guide to Giving" based upon Stephen Post's book, *The Hidden Gifts of Helping*. It should help spark some ideas:

LISTEN. *By simply being attentive, you're satisfying an important human need—to be heard. "As anyone's spouse will attest," says Post. "If you're not listening, you're not loving me." Listening to someone speak may be the greatest act of giving you do today.*

Try it: Hold back.
  Next time you're talking with your spouse, friend or child, make a concerted effort to let that person express his or her thoughts without interrupting. (It's harder than it sounds.)

ACT OUT. *Giving is a powerful antidote to negativity. "Emotions actually follow your actions," says Post. If you're feeling enraged, annoyed or just miffed, he says, engage in helping activities—and you'll turn off the neural circuits associated with destructive emotions.*

Try it: Shift gears.
  Next time you feel caught in a downward spiral of self-pity, act in a way that runs counter to your mood: Spring for coffee, play a

game with your kids, or reach out to someone whom you know is having a tougher day than you are.

GIVE IN PERSON. All types of giving confer benefits on the giver—but nothing is as rewarding as the face-to-face variety. "Giving in person has a whole other biological dynamic, involving higher production of oxytocin, a hormone associated with feelings of serenity and tranquility," says Post.

Try it: Show up.

Rather than only giving online, do some good deeds in person. When you ring a doorbell with flowers in hand, for instance, you enhance the experience for yourself and the recipient.

EMPOWER. Nurturing another person's growth is one of the highest orders of giving—and has been shown to protect and improve physical and mental health over a lifetime.

Try it: Take someone under your wing.

Whether this means assuming the role of mentor, or taking the new hire out to lunch, seek out ways to enable someone else to grow, and you'll have given a priceless gift.

Rumi, a thirteenth-century Persian mystic,
told of a man who walked past a beggar and asked,
"Why, God, do you not do something for these people?"
God replied, "I did do something. I made you."

~ from *The Power of Giving* by Azim Jamal and Harvey McKinnon

Your Time, Talent and Treasure:
DO YOUR PART TO CHANGE THE WORLD

Regardless of the size of our wallet or position in life, each of us can do our part to improve the world around us, by sharing our time, talents, and if we are lucky enough to have it, our treasure.

In his book, *Easier than You Think*, Dr. Richard Carlson shows us how to "Give a Little."

When Mother Teresa was asked how people could make themselves happier, she often responded, "Go out and serve someone." The truth is that nothing feels better than being generous. Conversely, nothing creates more spiritual emptiness than being stingy.

Obviously, everyone is in a different position when it comes to giving. While one person may be able to make a $10,000 gift with zero financial impact, someone else may be severely burdened by making a ten-dollar gift. Being stingy has nothing to do with the amount you give, but with the attitude and spirit in which you give it.

Being stingy, of course, extends far beyond the financial realm. We can be stingy with our time, our love, our ideas, and our willingness to be of help. We can even be stingy with our willingness to reach out to others or to forgive.

Spiritually, one thing is certain. When we step out of our comfort zone and give a little more than what we are accustomed to giving, be it money, love, time, ideas, forgiveness, or assistance, it comes back to us with interest.

Here's an example of how this small change brings big rewards.

My neighbor John came home from a business trip to India, where hungry children living on the street had reached out to beg for help at every turn. The experience made a big impression on him. John saw for the first time how every little bit makes a difference.

It had always been John's habit when he came home at night to gather his loose change and put it by his wallet, watch, and keys so he could use it the next day for the toll on his commute. But after his trip he started a new habit. He put a large glass jar next to his dresser. He then made a commitment to himself that every day after work, instead of saving the loose change for his own use; he would put it into the jar. Whether he had twenty-five cents or four dollars in change, he'd donate every last cent to the jar. When the jar was full, he rolled the coins, deposited them in the bank, and wrote a check for that amount to a charity that served children in developing countries. Just like that, John had found a way to become more generous.

I've talked to hundreds of people, from wealthy CEOs to teenagers who are former gang members, about giving more time and money. And I have never ever met a person who made the decision to do so and then later regretted it. In fact, in every case, a slight increase in generosity brought immense joy and meaning to that person's own life as well as to those he or she was able to help. So why not make the choice to give a little more? Small change goes a long way.

"I have found that among its other benefits,
giving liberates the soul of the giver."

~ Maya Angelou

USE YOUR TALENT TO CHANGE A LIFE

No matter what your profession, you have an opportunity to change the lives of those you work with. But, teachers have a special privilege—they have the opportunity to give of their talents to change the next generation. Internationally known author and speaker Wayne Dyer experienced that first-hand when a teacher reached out to help change the direction of his life. Here's his story of *A Teacher's Legacy*, excerpted from *Inspiration Your Ultimate Calling*:

I was inspired by Mrs. Olive Fletcher. In 1956, I was taking biology for the second time at Denby High School in Detroit. I'd failed the class the previous year because of my own stubbornness. I'd refused to complete a leaf collection, what my then 15-year-old self perceived it to be an absurd requirement.

> "YOU CAN GIVE WITHOUT LOVING, BUT YOU CAN NEVER LOVE WITHOUT GIVING."
>
> ~ *Robert Louis Stevenson*

At that time, my mother was divorcing my alcoholic step-father, and I was working evenings during the week and all day on Saturday and Sunday at a local grocery store. My instructor for this second foray into biology was Mrs. Fletcher, and she was the very first teacher I encountered who seemed to care about me personally. For example, she was there for me after school, called my home to see if I was okay during the tumultuousness (including frequent fights and other unpleasantness) taking place at the time, and allowed me to put my head down and sleep during study periods when I'd completed my assignments. She also encouraged me to tutor other students because she recognized something in me that I'd never heard a teacher say before: She told me that I was brilliant and had a mind that could take me wherever I wanted to go.

This incredible person even invited me to go bowling with her and her husband. Before I met Mrs. Fletcher, I'd never imagined that teachers were actually human, let alone went bowling. She was the first "authority figure" who welcomed my questioning and tolerated my sometimes disruptive behavior. She showed me that I was worthy of being loved by someone in a position of authority.

Thanks to Mrs. Fletcher's inspiration, I went from a failing grade the previous year to an A. I wanted to excel just for her because she had so much faith in me. Now, exactly a half-century later, Mrs. Olive Fletcher still stands out as the one individual in all of my school years who turned the direction of my life from fighting the system to being able to choose to fit in without having to give in.

"There are those whose hands have sunbeams
in them so that their grasp warms my heart."

~ *Helen Keller*

A LITTLE TIME CAN CHANGE YOUR WORLD...

In *The Generosity Plan*, author Kathy LeMay shares a story of how giving of your time and talent can make all the difference:

When Regina's husband, Alex, lost his job as a corporate consultant, the family leaned on her income. However, as the months wore on, their accounts began to dwindle. They revisited their budget and cut where they could.

Six months into his unemployment, Alex realized that Regina was still giving a monthly gift to their community center. Her husband said that while he cared about this center, they couldn't afford it. He said that for now, they just didn't have it in their budget. Regina pushed back, saying it was only $50 and it was important to do. Alex was angry and called her irresponsible. He said that you give when you are fine, and they, he stated, were not fine.

Regina wasn't sure what to do. She wanted to keep stress low in their family but also felt they owed something to their elders. So she asked her husband if they and their two daughters could volunteer at the center. He didn't love the idea, but she pushed and said it was important for the girls.

The next month, they joined other community members on the Saturday volunteer day for the center's art and bake sale. Regina and her daughters brought cookies, while the center provided paper and paints for the girls to draw on. They then sold the pictures at the same table as the beverages and baked goods. The girls loved it. They also made paintings for the seniors at the center and asked their parents if they could go every week.

As you can imagine, Alex changed his mind about the monthly gift. When he saw firsthand how each dollar was put to use to host arts and crafts and exercise programs for the seniors, he said it made a difference to see their money at work in support of senior citizens. He told his wife he wanted to set a good example for their daughters and felt they could make the $50 donation work.

As the months progressed, Regina, Alex and their daughters continued to volunteer. One Saturday, while talking with another volunteer, Alex shared that he was still looking for work. The other volunteer said he might know of something and he'd let him know. The following Saturday, the volunteer approached Alex and asked if he could interview that week at the company where he was employed. One month later, Alex had a job.

Staying connected to your community and giving back during difficult times won't guarantee you employment, but staying holed up inside your house certainly won't have you meeting people and knowing what opportunities are available. Later, Alex asked the other volunteer why he got him the interview. He said that any guy who would give of his time when he was looking for work was someone with the right work ethic for the company.

"Let us not be satisfied with just giving money. Money is not enough, money can be got, but they need your hearts to love them. So, spread your love everywhere you go."

~ *Mother Teresa*

"THERE IS NO HAPPINESS IN
HAVING OR IN GETTING,
BUT ONLY IN GIVING."

~ Henry Drummond

THE PARADOX OF *Giving:*
HOW GIVING GIVES BACK

Back in 1988, Alan Luks surveyed more than 3,000 volunteers of all ages throughout the country and documented the physical and emotional benefits of giving, including a full 50 percent who reported feeling a "helper's high" after helping others.

Since then, studies have shown that those who give to others experience increased health and happiness, and even a reduced mortality rate.

Cami Walker is someone who learned first-hand about how giving can be a two-way street. Here's her story as reported by Jessica Ravitz on CNN.com:

Cami Walker received a prescription to give when her multiple sclerosis, a diagnosis she got at age 33, left her a physical and emotional wreck.

She could barely get out of bed, and yet Mbali Creazzo, a friend and spiritual mentor, single-handedly killed Walker's pity party. She said, "'Cami, you really need to stop thinking about yourself. ... You're feeding this disease,'" Walker remembers. "She said, 'I have a prescription for you. Give away 29 gifts in 29 days.'"

Creazzo, a South-African born medicine woman who lives in Oakland, California, explained that the idea, rooted in indigenous practices, was taught to her, although the number of days prescribed may have been different.

"Altruism has been going on for thousands of years," said Creazzo, 58. "Why it's so powerful at this moment is because of what's happening in the world today. People are looking for that place inside of them where they are of some use."

Walker, who lives in Hollywood, California, dismissed Creazzo's suggestion at first but came back to it when she realized she had nothing to lose by trying. What followed made her a convert to the idea. Whether she simply called a friend to offer support or bought iced-tea for a homeless guy on a hot day, the simple actions made a difference. She said her mood lifted, her

The SECRET TO LIVING IS
GIVING

ability to get around improved and the progression of the disease stopped.

"I don't see it as a cure. I still have MS," said Walker, who went on to write the best-seller "29 Gifts: How a Month of Giving Can Change Your Life" and create an online community at 29gifts.org, where Creazzo is also involved. "I really don't think about the limitations of my disease. I wake up more focused on what I'm capable of."

"KINDNESS IN WORDS CREATES CONFIDENCE. KINDNESS IN THINKING CREATES PROFOUNDNESS. KINDNESS IN GIVING CREATES LOVE."

~ *Lao Tzu*

Now, nearly 5,000 people in 38 countries have committed themselves to the 29-Day Giving Challenge by signing up on the website at www.29Gifts.com. Here's just one example from Cami Walker's book:

A DIFFERENT WAY TO KEEP WARM

By Jennifer Meriposa Fuller

The wind whipped around me, a biting chill making its way through my clothes. It seemed that the sunny Portland, Oregon, summer had given way immediately to winter, with no mild autumn in-between. The weather had caught me off guard and I wasn't dressed for it, with only a thin sweater and jeans. To make matters worse, I had been talking to my friend for an hour on my cell phone, while sitting in the park, meaning that my right hand now was a frozen claw. "Hot chocolate!" I exclaimed excitedly to myself. That was exactly what I needed. I made my way to the nearest corner coffee shop and ordered a medium cocoa. Usually I would get the large, but money was extremely tight for me these days, being unemployed for almost a year, and buying this hot chocolate at all was a treat.

I emerged from the coffee shop with that enormous satisfaction you feel when you've just received the exact thing you had been craving. I crossed the street, wind howling at me from all directions. And just as I was about to take that first glorious sip, I spotted a woman to my left. She was homeless, sitting on the cold concrete holding a cardboard sign. The woman was bundled as best as she could against the weather, but I imagined she must be freezing. Without thinking, I immediately walked over to her. "Would you like some hot chocolate?" I asked, and held out the cup.

The pained expression on her face changed in an instant. Her eyes got wide and bright with surprise and anticipation, like a kid at Christmas. The excitement on her face was a million times more than the satisfaction I was feeling seconds before. "Oh yes, thank you!" she chirped at me. I gave it to

The SECRET TO LIVING IS
GIVING

her with a huge smile on my face and continued down the street. As I walked away, she buried her face in the steam and reveled in its warmth.

Suddenly, I wasn't so cold anymore. It was as if the giving of something so small and simple, yet completely delightfully received, had literally warmed my soul. And to top it off, I couldn't stop smiling. Immediately I wanted to do more, as if I wanted to spread the contagiousness of happiness around. I walked down the street looking for others to help. It was an eagerness that was almost obsessive, probably visible. The giving had just felt so good.

Then it hit me. I hadn't thought twice about giving her that hot chocolate, even though I had been craving it for myself for about an hour. The moment I saw the woman, I just knew that she needed it far more than I did, and I automatically handed it over. I realized that as I had been giving each day in the spirit of 29 Gifts, it had become second nature. I am so grateful that I got to experience the world around me in a different light, one that involves not only noticing others' desires but knowing that I have the ability to help fulfill them if I so choose. And that is a powerful thing.

"When I chased after money,
I never had enough.
When I got my life on purpose
and focused on giving of myself
and everything that arrived into my life,
then I was prosperous."

~Wayne Dyer

THE GIFT OF ENCOURAGEMENT

Giving comes in many different forms. One of the most powerful is...giving encouragement. In *The Power of a Note*, author Fred Bauer shows that it may be as simple as picking up a pen:

On my first job as sports editor for the Montpelier (Ohio) Leader Enterprise, I didn't get a lot of fan mail, so I was intrigued by a letter plopped on my desk one morning. The envelope bore the logo of the closest big-city paper, the Toledo Blade.

When I opened it, I read:

"Sweet piece of writing on the Tigers. Keep up the good work."

It was signed by Don Wolfe, the sports editor. Because I was a teenager (being paid the grand total of 15 cents a column inch), his words could not have been more exhilarating. I kept the letter in my desk drawer until it got rag-eared. Whenever I doubted I had the right stuff to be a writer, I would reread Don's note and walk on air again.

Later, when I got to know him, I learned that Don made a habit of jotting a quick, encouraging word to people in all walks of life. "When I make others feel good about themselves," he told me, "I feel good, too."

Why are upbeat note writers in such short supply? My guess is that many who shy away from the practice are too self-conscious. They are afraid they will be misunderstood, sound corny or fawning. Also, writing takes time and it is far easier to pick up the phone. The drawback with phone calls, of course, is that they do not last. A note attaches more importance to our well-wishing. It is a matter of record, and our words can be read more than once, savored and treasured.

What does it take to write notes that lift spirits and warm hearts? Perhaps just a desire and a willingness to express our appreciation. The most successful practitioners write notes that are short on verbiage and long on empathy; sincere, short, specific and usually spontaneous in nature.

It is difficult to be spontaneous, however, when you have to hunt for letter writing materials: so, keep paper, envelopes, and stamps close at hand, even when you travel. Fancy stationery is not necessary; it's the thought that counts.

So, who around you deserves a note of thanks or approval? A neighbor, your librarian, a relative, your mayor, your mate, a teacher or doctor? You do not need to be poetic. If you need a reason, look for a milestone, the anniversary of a special event you shared, a birthday, or holiday, and do not constrain your praise. Superlatives such as: "greatest," "smartest," "prettiest" make us all feel good. Even if your plaudits run a little ahead of reality, remember that expectations are often the parents of dreams fulfilled.

Today, I received a warm, complimentary letter from my old boss and mentor, Norman Vincent Peale. He once told me that the purpose of writing inspirational notes (he is the best three-sentence letter writer I have ever known) is simply "to build others up because there are too many people in the demolition business today."

His little note to me was full of uplifting phrases, and it sent me to my typewriter to compose a few overdue letters of my own. I don't know if they will make anybody else's day, but they made mine. As my friend Don Wolfe said, "Making others feel good about themselves makes me feel good, too."

"You never know when
one kind act, or one word
of encouragement,
can change a life forever."

~ Zig Ziglar

"It isn't the size of the gift that matters, but the size of the heart that gives it."

~ *Eileen Elias Freeman*

EXPERIENCE THE POWER OF GIVING

In their book, *The Power of Giving*, authors Azim Jamal and Harvey McKinnon summed up the paradox ... and the power of giving:

Giving creates a symbiotic relationship; it benefits both parties. The recipients benefit from your gift. And you benefit personally by virtue of having been a giver. Sometimes it is easy to see the immediate benefits to those you help. Other times, the ultimate benefits of your action may occur many years in the future. It could be that your gift helps the sick, funds a project for your favorite charity, or helps a child learn something valuable. Whatever your gift, your time, money, or effort will have a positive impact.

The other side of the equation is the benefits to you. They may be visible and immediate, or they may be intangible and delayed. You may not even recognize them as benefits. You may gain a tax deduction. You may feel great about your ability to help. You may receive heartfelt thanks. You may see the preservation of something you believe in or change in an area where you have been seeking it.

Whatever form the benefits take, giving brings meaning to your life. When you give, you have a chance to make an incredible impact during and often beyond your life. And when you give without expecting a return, you reap even more benefits.

Take the opportunity to make a difference in someone's life every day. Share your talents with others, give generously to those in need, and use the gift of your time to enrich the lives of others.

Together, we can change the world—because the *secret of living is giving.*

Giving

by BJ Gallagher

"It's better to give than receive,"
   my mother used to say.
      But it took some years
of experience
   before I fully understood
      what she meant.

When I gave my subway seat
   to an old lady,
      I felt kind.

When I dropped a dollar
   Into the street musician's hat,
      I felt generous.

When I let the harried driver
   cut in front of me on the road,
      I felt patient.

When I lent a hand
   to someone at work,
      I felt a part of the team.

When I brought a meal
   to my grieving neighbor,
      I felt empathetic.

When I gave some water
   to a thirsty dog.
      I felt happy.

When I wrote a check
    to a worthy cause
        I felt virtuous.

When I gave my friend
    the benefit of the doubt,
        I felt compassionate.

I discovered that
    when I give my time,
        my attention,
        my money,
        my thoughtfulness
    to another—
        I feel wonderful.

Mom was right ...
    it IS better to give
        than receive.

In giving,
    we generate warmth;

In giving,
    we feel connected;

In giving,
    we discover love.

About the Author

MAC ANDERSON is the founder of Simple Truths and Successories, Inc., the leader in designing and marketing products for motivation and recognition. These companies, however, are not the first success stories for Mac. He was also the founder and CEO of McCord Travel, the largest travel company in the Midwest, and part owner/VP of sales and marketing for Orval Kent Food Company, the country's largest manufacturer of prepared salads.

His accomplishments in these unrelated industries provide some insight into his passion and leadership skills. He also brings the same passion to his speaking where he speaks to many corporate audiences on a variety of topics, including leadership, motivation, and team building.

Mac has authored or co-authored eighteen books that have sold over four million copies. His titles include:

- *Change is Good ... You Go First*
- *Charging the Human Battery*
- *Customer Love*
- *Finding Joy*
- *Learning to Dance in the Rain*
- *212°: The Extra Degree*
- *212° Leadership*
- *212° Service*
- *Motivational Quotes*
- *One Choice*
- *The Nature of Success*
- *The Power of Attitude*
- The Power of Kindness
- *The Essence of Leadership*
- *The Road to Happiness*
- *The Dash*
- *To a Child, Love is Spelled T-I-M-E*
- *You Can't Send a Duck to Eagle School*
- *What's the Big Idea?*

For more information about Mac, visit *www.simpletruths.com*

What OTHERS are saying...

We purchased a Simple Truths' gift book for our conference in Lisbon, Spain. We also personalized it with a note on the first page about valuing innovation. I've never had such positive feedback on any gift we've given. People just keep talking about how much they valued the book and how perfectly it tied back to our conference message.

— **Michael R. Marcey,** Efficient Capital Management, LLC.

The small inspirational books by Simple Truths are amazing magic! They spark my spirit and energize my soul.

— **Jeff Hughes,** United Airlines

Mr. Anderson, ever since a friend of mine sent me the 212° movie online, I have become a raving fan of Simple Truths. I love and appreciate the positive messages your products convey and I have found many ways to use them. Thank you for your vision.

— **Patrick Shaughnessy,** AVI Communications, Inc.

simple truths®
Motivational & Inspirational Gifts

SMALL BOOKS THAT SPEAK VOLUMES

Be sure to enjoy our complete collection of e-books. You'll discover it's a great way to inspire friends and family, or to thank your best customers and employees.

For more information, please visit us at:

www.simpletruths.com
Or call us toll free… 800-900-3427

"Never get tired of doing little things for others, sometimes those little things occupy the biggest parts of their hearts."

~ Unknown